M000284368

WHAT I LOVE ABOUT
Me

WHAT I LOVE ABOUT

Me

A BOOK TO
PERSONALISE
FOR YOU

A STUDIO PRESS BOOK

First published in the UK in 2022 by Studio Press,
an imprint of Bonnier Books UK
4th Floor, Victoria House
Bloomsbury Square, London WC1B 4DA
Owned by Bonnier Books
Sveavägen 56, Stockholm, Sweden

www.bonnierbooks.co.uk

© 2022 Studio Press

1 3 5 7 9 10 8 6 4 2

All rights reserved
ISBN 978-1-80078-283-9

Written by Ellie Rose
Designed by Rob Ward and Wendy Bartlet
Production by Emma Kidd

A CIP catalogue record for this book is available from the British Library
Printed and bound in China

Celebrate your past, present and future
and create a book that is all about you.

The most important relationship in your life is the
one you have with yourself. This book will help you to
reflect on your life, work, love and relationships and
encourage you to celebrate all you have achieved.

You are unique and wonderful and
this book will remind you of that!

This book belongs to

Taking the time every day to write down your thoughts and feelings is a great way to check in with yourself and track your progress over time.

Good morning!

Today, I am grateful for…

1 ....

2 ....

3 ....

I will invest my time and energy into…

1 ....

2 ....

Write your daily affirmation.
I am…

....

....

....

Write your answers to the prompts below, then use it as a template to create your own personalised daily journal.

Goodnight!

Today, these amazing things happened...

1 ....

2 ....

3 ....

What could I have done to make today even better?

....

....

....

What will I improve tomorrow?

....

....

....

....

At the end of the week, take a moment to sit and reflect.
Answer the questions and then use this as a template to
track your weeks over time.

What are my current priorities, and did I fulfil them this
week?

....

....

This week, I spent too much time…

....

....

This week, I didn't spend enough time…

....

....

What surprised me this week?

....

....

....

....

This week, I am grateful for…

1 ....

2 ....

3 ....

Use this space to write any thoughts or feelings that came up throughout the course of the week.

....

....

....

....

Use this space to celebrate any successes this week.

....

....

....

....

Set your ambitions for the month ahead and, once the month is complete, reflect on the highs and lows.

Date: _____   _____ 20_____

My goals for the month ahead

1 ....

2 ....

3 ....

I will invest my time and energy into…

....

....

....

....

This month I will make time for…

....

....

....

....

....

Use this as a template to track how you feel from month to month and appreciate what you have achieved.

Date: _____   _____ 20_____

How did I meet my goals this month?

....

....

What went well this month?

....

....

What can I improve for next month?

....

....

This month I am grateful for…

I ....

2 ....

3 ....

Monthly Reflection

On a scale of 0-10, rate yourself in each of the following categories:

(0 = lowest mark, 10 = highest mark)

Gratitude ☐

Happiness ☐

Friendships ☐

Physical health ☐

Work or education ☐

Fun ☐

Creativity ☐

Finances ☐

Mindfulness ☐

Mental health ☐

Free time ☐

Exercise and movement ☐

Use this space to write down your overall thoughts and feelings for the month.

....

....

....

....

....

....

....

....

....

....

....

Fill in the habits you would like to build over time and then tick the box every day you complete them.

Habit	1	2	3	4	5	6	7	8	9	10	11	12	13
Fill in daily journal	☐	☐	☐	☐	☐	☐	☐	☐	☐	☐	☐	☐	☐
	☐	☐	☐	☐	☐	☐	☐	☐	☐	☐	☐	☐	☐
	☐	☐	☐	☐	☐	☐	☐	☐	☐	☐	☐	☐	☐
	☐	☐	☐	☐	☐	☐	☐	☐	☐	☐	☐	☐	☐
	☐	☐	☐	☐	☐	☐	☐	☐	☐	☐	☐	☐	☐
	☐	☐	☐	☐	☐	☐	☐	☐	☐	☐	☐	☐	☐
	☐	☐	☐	☐	☐	☐	☐	☐	☐	☐	☐	☐	☐
	☐	☐	☐	☐	☐	☐	☐	☐	☐	☐	☐	☐	☐
	☐	☐	☐	☐	☐	☐	☐	☐	☐	☐	☐	☐	☐
	☐	☐	☐	☐	☐	☐	☐	☐	☐	☐	☐	☐	☐
	☐	☐	☐	☐	☐	☐	☐	☐	☐	☐	☐	☐	☐
	☐	☐	☐	☐	☐	☐	☐	☐	☐	☐	☐	☐	☐

Use this as a template to create your own monthly habit tracker.

14	15	16	17	18	19	20	21	22	23	24	25	26	27	28	29	30	31
☐	☐	☐	☐	☐	☐	☐	☐	☐	☐	☐	☐	☐	☐	☐	☐	☐	☐
☐	☐	☐	☐	☐	☐	☐	☐	☐	☐	☐	☐	☐	☐	☐	☐	☐	☐
☐	☐	☐	☐	☐	☐	☐	☐	☐	☐	☐	☐	☐	☐	☐	☐	☐	☐
☐	☐	☐	☐	☐	☐	☐	☐	☐	☐	☐	☐	☐	☐	☐	☐	☐	☐
☐	☐	☐	☐	☐	☐	☐	☐	☐	☐	☐	☐	☐	☐	☐	☐	☐	☐
☐	☐	☐	☐	☐	☐	☐	☐	☐	☐	☐	☐	☐	☐	☐	☐	☐	☐
☐	☐	☐	☐	☐	☐	☐	☐	☐	☐	☐	☐	☐	☐	☐	☐	☐	☐
☐	☐	☐	☐	☐	☐	☐	☐	☐	☐	☐	☐	☐	☐	☐	☐	☐	☐
☐	☐	☐	☐	☐	☐	☐	☐	☐	☐	☐	☐	☐	☐	☐	☐	☐	☐
☐	☐	☐	☐	☐	☐	☐	☐	☐	☐	☐	☐	☐	☐	☐	☐	☐	☐
☐	☐	☐	☐	☐	☐	☐	☐	☐	☐	☐	☐	☐	☐	☐	☐	☐	☐
☐	☐	☐	☐	☐	☐	☐	☐	☐	☐	☐	☐	☐	☐	☐	☐	☐	☐

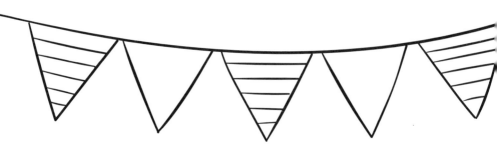

My intentions for the year ahead

I want to quit: ....

....

I want to learn: ....

....

I want to try: ....

....

I want to have: ....

....

I want to start: ....

....

I want to continue: ....

....

I'm going to stop: ....

....

I want to be: ....

....

What would I do if there was no way to fail?

Six months

Be: ....

....

....

Do: ....

....

....

Have: ....

....

....

12 months

Be: ....

....

....

Do: ....

....

....

Have: ....

....

....

My goals for the year ahead

Personal

1 ....

2 ....

3 ....

4 ....

Health

1 ....

2 ....

3 ....

4 ....

Career

1 ....

2 ....

3 ....

4 ....

Recreational

1 ....

2 ....

3 ....

4 ....

Home

1 ....

2 ....

3 ....

4 ....

....

1 ....

2 ....

3 ....

4 ....

My Affirmations

I am…

My Affirmations

I am…

....

....

....

....

....

....

....

....

My Past

I was born in

....

I grew up in

....

....

I went to primary school in

....

....

I went to high school in

....

....

My favourite teacher

....

....

My favourite school subjects

....

....

....

....

....

My first best friend

....

....

....

My first pet

....

....

....

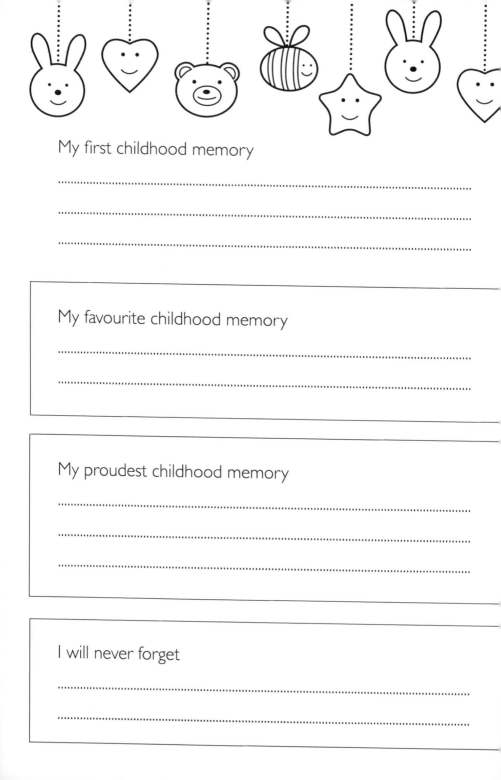

My first childhood memory

....

....

....

My favourite childhood memory

....

....

My proudest childhood memory

....

....

....

I will never forget

....

....

I would tell my younger self…

....

....

....

My favourite hobby

....

....

....

I wish I had been more

....

....

....

I wish I had been less

....

....

....

Personal Relationships

Are there any relationships in my life I would like to improve?

....

....

....

Are there any relationships in my life that would benefit from forgiveness?

....

....

....

How can I positively influence others?

....

....

....

How can I better communicate with others?

....

....

....

What are three things I can do for myself every week?

1 ....

2 ....

3 ....

How can I improve my relationship with myself?

....

....

....

Is there anything I would like to forgive myself for?

....

....

....

My relationship with my mother is…

....

....

My relationship with my father is…

....

....

I would describe my family as…

....

....

....

....

....

....

My favourite family members

....

....

I am closest to…

....

....

....

If I were to have children, what would I repeat from my childhood?

....

....

What would I change?

....

....

First Time for Everything

My first friend ....

The first song I bought ....
....

My first holiday ....
....

The first live music I saw ....
....

My first kiss ....

My first love ....
....

My first pet ....

My first day at school ....
....

My first job ....
....

Food I recently tried for the first time ....
....

My most recent first ....
....

The next thing I want to do for the first time ....
....
....

Don't Overthink

Write the first thing that pops into your mind – did any of your answers surprise you?

I want to travel to ....

I want to eat ....

I want to drink ....

I wish I could ....

Today I feel ....

I'm thinking about ....

I regret ....

I don't regret ....

Tomorrow I will ....

I've been putting off ....

I would change ....

I would keep ....

I hate ....

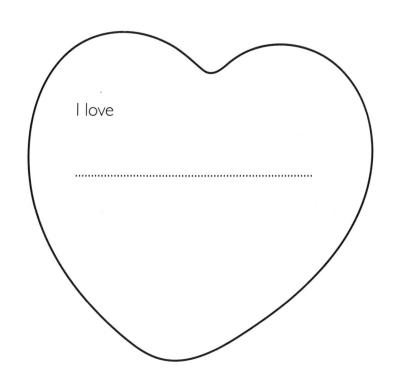

I love

....

Fun and Celebration

What's one way I could have more fun?

....

....

....

Where would I like to go on holiday?

....

....

....

What gift would I give myself?

....

....

....

What gift would I like to give someone else?

....

....

....

....

How do I want to celebrate my next birthday?

....

....

....

If I threw a themed party, what would the theme be?

....

....

....

If I could throw a surprise party for someone, who would
it be for? Why?

....

....

....

If I could have dinner with three people in history,
alive or dead, who would I invite?

1 ....

2 ....

3 ....

Our work can take up a lot of our time and energy so use this space to reflect on how this makes you feel.

Things I enjoy about my work

....

....

....

Things I don't enjoy about my work

....

....

....

Where I see myself in...

I year ....

....

3 years ....

....

5 years ....

....

If I could start again, what would I do the same?

....

....

What would I change?

....

....

Someone I admire is

....

I admire them because

....

....

My dream job would be

....

....

What made me think hard today and why?

....

....

....

....

....

....

....

....

....

Did I work as hard as I could have? If not, why not? How can I improve next time?

....

....

....

....

....

....

....

....

What are my strengths and how can I use them in my life? ....

....

....

....

....

What are my weaknesses and how do I overcome them in my life? ....

....

....

....

....

What is my biggest accomplishment this week?
In my lifetime? ....

....

....

....

....

What is my biggest fear? What can I do to
overcome this? ....

....

....

....

....

....

....

What are three things I can do today that will make me
happy?

1 ....

....

....

2 ....

....

....

3 ....

....

....

Write three positive affirmations I will say every day
for a month:

1 ....

....

2 ....

....

3 ....

....

What is something I did today that I can celebrate as a

success? ....

....

....

Write three things I loved about today:

1 ....

....

2 ....

....

3 ....

....

Personal Style

My style in three words

1 ....

2 ....

3 ....

Is there anything I would change about my style?

....

....

....

....

....

....

....

My three style icons

1 ....

2 ....

3 ....

My dream outfit is

....

....

....

A hairstyle I'd like to try

....

....

....

If I were to dye my hair, I would choose

....

My opinion of piercings

....

....

....

My opinion of tattoos

....

....

....

I would describe my personality as

1 ....

2 ....

3 ....

4 ....

I think other people would describe my personality as

1 ....

2 ....

3 ....

4 ....

One thing I would change about myself is

....

....

I think people's first impression of me is

....

....

....

I love this about myself

....

....

....

I am secretly envious of

....

....

My biggest fear is

....

....

....

....

How do I make a difference in the lives of those around me?

....

....

....

....

I wish I could…

....

....

....

....

What causes or charities am I passionate about?

....

....

....

....

....

You MATTER
We CARE
You are not alone

Mental Health Peer Support
for mums and birthing people

LATNEM

 latnempeersupport

latnem7

 hello@latnem.org

latnem.org

 latnempeersupport

Who is someone making a difference that I admire?

....

....

....

....

....

What can I learn from them?

....

....

....

....

....

What is one small thing I could do every day to make

a difference?

....

....

....

....

Digital World

Guess how long, on average, you spend on your phone every day.

....

If your phone shows your usage per day, have a look.
Did the numbers surprise you?

....

....

Do I spend a good amount of time on my phone or too much time?

....

....

Do I use my phone to waste time during the day?

....

....

What would I rather spend time doing?

....

....

....

....

Steps I can put in place to prevent overuse of my phone

....

....

....

....

....

....

....

....

....

....

....

Use this space to reflect on all you have achieved and take a moment to congratulate yourself.

What is something I have recently achieved that I can celebrate as a success?

....

....

....

....

The thing I am most proud of personally is

....

....

....

The thing I am most proud of professionally is

....

....

....

....

People told me I could never

....

....

....

I was scared to

....

....

....

.... but I did it anyway.

People often celebrate the success of others more than their own successes. Put yourself in someone else's shoes – what about you would impress them?

....

....

....

....

....

....

Sometimes it's good to sit back and remember all of the fun times we've had. Tick the box next to anything you have done in the past and then add in your own favourite memories.

Been camping ☐

Ridden a horse ☐

Gone skinny dipping ☐

Seen a live show ☐

Stayed up all night ☐

Got a tattoo ☐

Been to a festival ☐

Dyed my hair ☐

Kissed a stranger ☐

Skipped work to do something fun ☐

Worn an outrageous outfit ☐

Danced on stage ☐

Fallen madly in love ☐

Taken a spontaneous trip ☐

Laughed till I cried ☐

Got a piercing ☐

Visited a casino ☐

Made friends with a stranger ☐

Snuck in somewhere I shouldn't have ☐

Did something that scared me ☐

.... ☐

.... ☐

.... ☐

Note down the last time you…

Laughed ....

Cried ....

Felt happy ....

Felt angry ....

Ate ....

Drank water ....

Watched a film ....

Read a book ....

Said I love you ....

Said thank you ....

Failed ....

Succeeded ....

Lied ....

Told the truth ....

Spoke to my family ....

Saw my friends ....

Did something that scared me ....

Went on an adventure

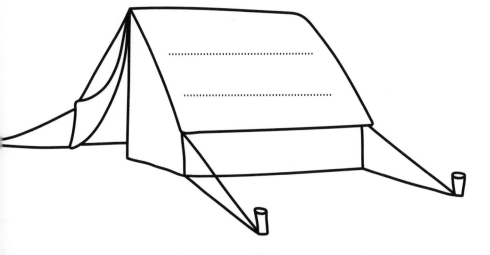

Which do you prefer? Tick your preference.

☐	Bath	or	Shower	☐
☐	Beach	or	Mountain	☐
☐	Hot	or	Cold	☐
☐	Sunrise	or	Sunset	☐
☐	Book	or	Film	☐
☐	Pizza	or	Pasta	☐
☐	Fast	or	Slow	☐
☐	Sing	or	Dance	☐
☐	Cat	or	Dog	☐

☐	Walk	or	Run	☐
☐	Night in	or	Night out	☐
☐	Quiet	or	Loud	☐
☐	Text	or	Call	☐
☐	Home	or	Abroad	☐
☐	Lake	or	Ocean	☐
☐	Music	or	Podcast	☐
☐	Food	or	Drink	☐
☐	Money	or	Love	☐
☐	Flowers	or	Plants	☐
☐	City	or	Countryside	☐

Room for Improvement

What new type of exercise or movement would I like to incorporate into my routine?

....

....

....

....

What types of food would I like to incorporate more of in my diet?

....

....

Are there any health appointments or priorities I have been putting off?

....

....

....

....

Are there any activities I can incorporate into my daily routine to help manage stress?

....

....

....

Write three health goals

1 ....

2 ....

3 ....

My body is amazing! Write down everything I love and are grateful for about my body.

....

....

....

....

....

....

Choose five items that mean something to you from each category.

Books

1 ....

2 ....

3 ....

4 ....

5 ....

Plays or Musicals

1 ....

2 ....

3 ....

4 ....

5 ....

Films

1 ....

2 ....

3 ....

4 ....

5 ....

Songs

1 ....

2 ....

3 ....

4 ....

5 ....

Albums

1 ....

2 ....

3 ....

4 ....

5 ....

Bands or Artists

1 ....

2 ....

3 ....

4 ....

5 ....

Podcasts

1 ....

2 ....

3 ....

4 ....

5 ....

Cities

1 ....

2 ....

3 ....

4 ....

5 ....

Holidays

1 ....

2 ....

3 ....

4 ....

5 ....

Friends

1 ....

2 ....

3 ....

4 ....

5 ....

Meals to Cook

1 ....

2 ....

3 ....

4 ....

5 ....

Inspirational people

1 ....

2 ....

3 ....

4 ....

5 ....

Self Care

When was the last time I took some time for myself?

....

....

....

....

Do I enjoy spending time alone?

....

My favourite way to relax

....

....

....

....

My favourite self-care activities

....

....

....

....

....

What self-care routines can I incorporate into my daily life?

....

....

....

....

In my perfect evening alone, what would I do?

....

....

....

....

....

....

....

....

....

....

Now schedule a date night with yourself – you deserve it!

One thing I can do to give myself more peace financially

....

....

....

A realistic amount of money would I like to save in the next year is

....

How will I achieve this goal?

....

....

....

Do I have any debt I would like to reduce or pay off?

....

....

....

....

....

What steps can I take to achieve this?

....

....

....

What are my long-term financial goals?

....

....

....

What do I need to do to achieve them?

....

....

....

Are there any charities or non-profit organisations I would like to support?

....

....

....

What advice would I give my younger self?

....

....

....

....

What is the biggest risk I've ever taken?

....

....

....

....

What risk would I most like to take?

....

....

....

....

What brings me joy?

....

....

....

....

How can I do more of what makes me happy?

....

....

....

....

What's one thing I would like to complete in the next
six months?

....

....

....

....

What do I need to do to achieve it?

....

....

....

....

What is my biggest talent?

....

....

....

Write your answer to each question and then ask why?

If I was a book, I would be…

....

If I was a film, I would be…

....

If I was a song, I would be…

....

If I was an animal, I would be…

....

If I was a flower,
I would be…

....

....

If I was a food, I would be…

....

....

If I was a tree, I would be…

....

If I was a celebrity, I would be…

....

If I was a colour, I would be…

....

If I was an emotion, I would be…

....

Friends Are Your Chosen Family

My closest friends are

....

....

My favourite thing to do with my friends is

....

....

....

Are my friends genuine?

....

....

Do my friends make me feel happy?

....

....

How do I make a positive impact on my friends?

....

....

....

....

How do my friends have a positive impact on me?

....

....

....

Do I trust my friends?

....

....

....

The last time I made a friend was

....

....

What do you dream of doing before it's too late?
Add your own wishes to the list.

Travel the world ☐

Learn a new language ☐

Run a marathon ☐

Sky dive ☐

Raise money for charity ☐

Get a tattoo ☐

Perform to a crowd ☐

Write a book ☐

Play a musical instrument ☐

Take a road trip ☐

If someone was to make a movie of my life…

I would be played by: ....
....
....

The supporting cast would be:

.... playing ....

.... playing ....

.... playing ....

.... playing ....

.... playing ....

.... playing ....

.... playing ....

The theme tune would be: ....
....

The soundtrack would include

1 ....

2 ....

3 ....

4 ....

5 ....

6 ....

The genre would be: ....
....
....

Room for Improvement

What mistakes have I made recently?

....

....

....

....

....

What have I learned from these experiences?

....

....

....

What would I do differently next time?

....

....

....

....

....

What skill can I learn that will have an impact on
my life?

....

....

....

Podcasts I would like to listen to

....

....

....

Books I would like to read

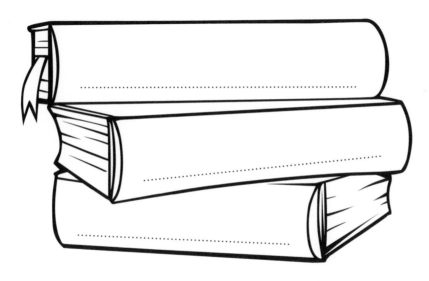

Vision for the Future

In one month, I will ....

....

....

In one year, I will ....

....

....

....

In five years, I will ....

....

....

....

In ten years, I will ....

....

....

....

What are the specific steps I need to achieve for my vision to come true? ....

....

....

....

....

....

....

How can I make myself accountable for my goals and vision? ....

....

....

....

....

....

....

Ten things I like about myself

1 ....

2 ....

3 ....

4 ....

5 ....

6 ....

7 ....

8 ....

9 ....

10 ....

What are three things that make me special?

1 ....

2 ....

3 ....

How have I pushed myself to grow recently?

....

....

What will I do to challenge myself this week?

....

....

....

How can I push myself out of my comfort zone?

....

....

....

I will forgive myself for

1 ....

2 ....

3 ....

What am I holding on to that I can't let go?

....

....

....

....

....

Use this space to write a letter to your past self:

....

....

....

....

....

....

....

....

....

Use this space to write a letter to your future self:

Make a list of the things that are most important to you.

··

··

··

··

··

··

Why are these things important?

··

··

··

What does love mean to me?

CONGRATULATIONS!

You have completed the book and hopefully have a new-found love and appreciation for YOU!

What have I learned about myself?

....

....

....

....

....

....

....

....

What do I love about myself?

....

....

....

....

....

....

....

....

....

....

What am I proud of?

....

....

....

....

....

....

....

....

....

....

What will I continue to do to make myself feel good?

....

....

....

....

....

....

....

....

....

....